CREATIVE WRITING PROMPTS FOR KIDS

SUITABLE FOR 9-13-YEAR-OLDS

SIMPLIFIED EDUCATION

HOW TO USE THIS WORKBOOK

HOW TO USE THIS WORKBOOK

- Grab a pen and lined paper
- Get a timer
- Read and understand the writing prompt
- Copy and write the prompt on your paper
- Read the example/guide answer
- Underline any unfamiliar vocabulary and check its meaning for a better understanding
- There will be an 'over to you' section after each guide answer
- Complete each 'over to you' section

- Back to your paper, plan for 5 minutes on what information you will include in your story
- Set your timer for 15 minutes after planning and start writing
- Only use the model answers as your guide or inspiration- you must not copy it
- There are no right or wrong answers but read each task carefully and respond correctly.
- Each task is different. Only write what's required.
- You can write as many versions as you want
- Read your work out loud and edit it for any mistakes
- Ask someone to read your work and ask them to give you an honest opinion.
- Enjoy and have fun.

EXAMPLE PAGE

Write a story which features the stopping of time.

Example/Guide Answer

I remember the daytime stopped like it was yesterday. I had been playing tag with a group of friends in the park, and we were having so much fun. Everyone was laughing and running around, completely unaware that something strange was about to happen.

OVER TO YOU!

Grab your pen and paper and have a go at writing your story. Remember to read and understand the task. Plan your writing, set your timer, and then you're ready to write. Have fun.

CREATIVE WRITING NUMBER 1

The Broken Window

Example/Guide Answer

I remember the day the window broke. It was a sunny afternoon, and I had been playing with my friends in our back garden when suddenly we heard a loud crash coming from the house. We rushed inside to find that one of our windows had shattered, leaving broken glass all over the floor. My heart sank as I realised what had happened.

We froze in place, unsure of what had just happened. Racing the door, we opened it to find glass everywhere. Our beautiful window was destroyed, and we couldn't figure out why. It wasn't windy outside, so it couldn't have been a gust of wind that caused the damage. I quickly looked around for something that might have hit it, but there was nothing nearby for miles. Whatever could have caused this damage?

My parents were both furious and disappointed at the same time. After assessing the damage, they determined that it must have been caused by an errant ball thrown during our game in the garden. The cost of replacing it would be high, so they took away some of my pocket money until they could afford to repair it.

CREATIVE WRITING NUMBER 2

The Abandoned House

Example/Guide Answer

I remember the first time I ever walked up to an abandoned house. I was so scared; my heart raced in anticipation as I tiptoed through the tall grass surrounding it, cautiously peeking through all its windows. Every step I took seemed to be amplified by the stillness of the night air as I approached it. As I got closer, I began to tiptoe, looking through its windows with curiosity and fear intertwined. Would anyone be inside? What would happen if they did catch me peeking?

My heart raced with anticipation and excitement as I creaked open the door. It was like stepping into a different world; everything inside seemed to be frozen in time. The sun had just begun to set and bathed the sky in a beautiful pink hue. When I finally opened the door, my palms started sweating profusely, and my knees quivered with excitement. The furniture sat dusty and untouched, and cobwebs hung from the ceiling. The walls were covered with peeling wallpaper that had seen better days.

Exploring this place felt almost magical, like walking through a fairy tale. I could see why it had been left for so long - it was eerie yet fascinating all at once! Even though no people lived in this house, I could feel their presence lingering everywhere I went. There were signs of family life around - from children's toys to boxes of old photos - which made me wonder what life must have been like here before they moved away.

CREATIVE WRITING NUMBER 3

The Lost Boy

Example/Guide Answer

I used to be a lost boy. I remember being scared, alone and confused about the world. Everywhere I looked, unfamiliar faces and voices spoke languages I didn't understand. All I wanted was to go back home - where everyone knew my name and loved me unconditionally, where I felt safe even when the night sky was so dark and filled with stars. But instead of returning home, I had tears rolling down my face because everything seemed strange.

I remember feeling like no one could help me or show me how to find my way home; it was as if all hope was lost for me ever getting back there again. All around me, I saw strange and unfamiliar surroundings that I had never seen before. Everywhere I looked, the scenery changed, yet nothing seemed familiar to me. My fear began to rise with no idea of where I was or how to get home.

I felt alone and scared in a place that wasn't mine; every step I took brought more worry and confusion as nothing made sense anymore. My heart raced with anxiety as tears filled my eyes; I only wanted a friendly face to show me how to return home safely. But no one was around—just an endless sea of faceless people walking by without a care.

CREATIVE WRITING NUMBER 4

The Voice in the Darkness

Example/Guide Answer

The voice in the darkness may be scary, but it can also bring wisdom and understanding. When I was little, my parents would take me camping out in the woods on our family trips.

I remember it like it was yesterday; I felt helpless, lost in the world with no hope of ever feeling safe again. I was scared and unsure of myself, not knowing what to do or how to get through this moment. But then something inside me changed; it started as a small whisper, but soon that whisper grew into a strong voice that filled every inch of my being.

As the sun set and we prepared for bed, the darkness of night slowly crept upon us. My heart started racing as I heard mysterious sounds from around us. When my dad switched on his torch to investigate, he found nothing - just the glare of moonlight reflecting off trees and shadows dancing in between them. But then there was something else - a voice from deep within the forest that seemed to whisper to me: "Be brave", said softly yet firmly.

This voice gave me courage when I thought it was gone forever; it reassured me with its calm yet confident presence. It told me everything would be okay if I kept going and never looked back.

CREATIVE WRITING NUMBER 5

The Garden

Example/Guide Answer

I have a special place in the world: my garden. It's where I can go to play and relax. When I'm there, I don't have to worry about anything else except what nature offers me. The garden has everything from trees with long branches to colourful flowers of all shapes and sizes. I love walking through it in the morning when the sun is barely coming up or seeing how different everything looks during sunset when all the colours are so vibrant!

My garden is a special place for me. It's my little piece of the world, where I can go to get away from it all and be. When I'm in my garden, nothing else matters. All the stress of school and other things fades away, and I can relax. The sweet smell of the flowers fills me with joy as soon as I step foot into my secret garden. Sometimes, when it rains, I lie down and let the droplets hit my face while listening to the gentle pitter-patter on the leaves above me.

My garden also provides refuge for many animals, like birds, squirrels, and butterflies. They come from far away because they know this is a place where they can eat without worrying about being disturbed or chased away. Watching them explore and play brings me so much joy and reminds me just how connected we are with nature!

Exploring around in my garden is one of my favourite activities too!

CREATIVE WRITING NUMBER 6

Sleeping

Example/Guide Answer

Sleep is one of my favourite things. When I get in my bed and pull the covers up to my chin, I feel so cosy and happy! I love dreaming about adventures with animals, flying, or visiting distant lands. It's like a mini escape from reality for a few hours. Sleep also helps me recharge after a busy day at school.

After I wake up, I feel refreshed and ready to tackle whatever tasks come next. Sleeping is important for overall health, too; doctors recommend getting 8-9 hours of sleep every night so our brains can rest and restore energy levels. The best thing about sleeping, though? No matter how tired I am during the day, just knowing that bedtime is close by always gives me an extra burst of energy to finish what needs to be done!

One of the best things about sleeping is that it's a chance to relax and unwind. I can snuggle up in my bed, close my eyes, and forget all my worries for a few hours. I don't have to worry about chores, school, or anything else when I'm asleep. It's like time stops for me, and I get to break from the world.

I also love dreaming when I sleep because sometimes you can be in entirely different worlds. In my dreams, I can explore new places and meet interesting people. Sometimes they are people I know in real life, but they act differently than usual - it's fun! And sometimes, they are characters that only exist in my head, so it almost feels like make-believe come to life.

CREATIVE WRITING NUMBER 7

The day the storm came

Example/Guide Answer

The day the storm came was unlike any other. The sky had been a bright, cheery blue all morning, with no cloud. But, out of nowhere, fluffy white clouds started rolling in from the horizon. I watched them curiously as they quickly filled the sky and made it look like a giant cotton ball. Then, as if someone had pushed a button, the rain started pouring down from the heavens. It seemed louder and faster than any rain I'd ever heard.

The thunder was crashing outside, and I could feel the reverberations of each clap throughout my body.

Even though it was pouring buckets, I couldn't help but be excited by the storm. The rumbling in the clouds made me feel alive, and I watched from my window as the lightning bolted through the sky.

I opened my window and stuck out my head as far as it would go. The raindrops were hitting me hard on the face, but that didn't matter - this was something special. Something beautiful! As if each drop was a sign of what's to come in life - good or bad. This moment felt like magic; it felt like anything could happen with such an overwhelming sound around me.

I couldn't help but be fascinated by what was happening around me. Lightning flashed an eerie light across the landscape, and thunder rumbled so loud that I thought it would shake my house apart! I knew this storm was not ordinary; its power truly scared me.

CREATIVE WRITING NUMBER 8

The day the weather changed

Example/Guide Answer

The day the weather changed was spectacular. I had been waiting for that day for so long, and when it finally arrived, I couldn't believe my eyes. The sun shone brighter than ever before, and a cool breeze blew across my face. Suddenly, the sky was filled with reds, oranges, purples, and blues. I jumped up in excitement as if this were a dream come true. It felt like something magical was happening right in front of me.

A cool breeze swept across my skin as I stepped outside, and I heard birds chirping in the distance.

A rainbow formed in the sky, bright colours reaching as far as my eyes could see. The smell of freshly cut grass filled the air, and butterflies danced around in circles - it was almost magical.

My family joined me in awe at what we saw outside our windows; it seemed as if every person could feel the excitement in the air. We all ran out to play together, feeling the energy running through us while admiring the beauty of our new surroundings. Everything felt alive!

CREATIVE WRITING NUMBER 9

A sunny day out

Example/Guide Answer

A sunny day out is so much fun! I love feeling the sun's warmth on my skin and seeing all the vibrant colours of nature. The sky is a bright blue, and puffy white clouds float around. The flowers look so pretty, with their petals shining in the sunshine. Some insects, like bees, have a good time flying around and gathering pollen. It's nice to sit back and enjoy the peacefulness of it all too.

On a sunny day, nothing is better than getting outside and soaking up the sun's warmth. I love when the sunshine glitters down on me, and it's so calming to feel the gentle breeze blowing across my face. I always have lots of fun these days because I can do many outdoor activities like playing tag with my friends or riding a bike. Whenever I'm out in the sun, it instantly brightens my mood and puts me in an adventurous mindset.

I also like playing outdoors when it's sunny outside too! Running around in a park or riding a bike along the beach can be exciting activities that make me feel alive and energised. Swimming in the ocean can be fun, too, especially when I can feel its refreshing waters after being out in hot weather for a while.

CREATIVE WRITING NUMBER 10

A foggy (or misty) day

Example/Guide Answer

Fog is one of the most mysterious things. It can be so thick that you can hardly see anything around you. On a foggy day, I love to go outside and explore. It's like stepping into another world; everything is so quiet and still in a way that I don't think I've ever experienced.

Everything is so still and quiet; the small droplets of water can be heard as they settle on the grass and leaves. The trees look like they're part of a dream, and everything has a hazy sort of glow to it. It's always so peaceful, just me and nature walking around together in our private world.

I can see things with fresh eyes since familiar sights no longer surround me. Even though I know my neighbourhood well, when there's fog, it looks so different that it feels novel again. Nothing compares to the feeling of stepping into this mysterious place, where anything could be hiding behind every corner or within every tree trunk!

One time, when it was foggy out, I saw the sun start to rise above the trees. Everything was illuminated with an orange light that made me feel so content and happy inside. As if nothing else mattered at that moment but the beauty of this scene in front of me. Even though it only lasted a few moments before it faded into the fog, I will never forget how precious this moment felt to me.

CREATIVE WRITING NUMBER 11

A day trip to remember

Example/Guide Answer

I remember that day like it was just yesterday. I had been excitedly counting the days until our family trip to the beach for what felt like forever. It was finally the day we were all looking forward to. We woke up bright and early and hit the road with enthusiasm. I scrambled out of bed with energy and ran around my room, filling up my suitcase with all my clothes and swimming gear. After packing, we jumped in the car and drove off on an adventure. The anticipation kept building as each mile passed; I couldn't wait to get there!

First, we stopped in town for breakfast at a local diner. We ordered pancakes, eggs, bacon, and toast — delicious! After that, we drove to the beach. The sound of waves crashing against rocks filled my ears as soon as I stepped out of the car—it was so calming and peaceful. My eyes lit up when I saw all the seashells glittering in the sunlight on the shoreline.

When we eventually arrived at the beach, it was even more amazing than I could have imagined! People played football on one side of the beach, and children splashed in puddles on another.

We played games on the sand while listening to music wafting through our headphones. This is indeed a day trip to remember.

CREATIVE WRITING NUMBER 12

The day everything changed

Example/Guide Answer

The day everything changed was a typical day, like any other. As usual, I woke up and got ready for school. At breakfast, my mum said that today would be different, but she wouldn't tell me why. When we arrived at school, something felt different. All my friends were gathered on the playground, whispering about something important.

I found out quickly enough what all this was about: our teacher had announced that he was leaving and that a new teacher would take his place soon. I couldn't believe it! How could this happen? He had been my teacher for the past four years, and I had grown so fond of him in such a short amount of time. I was sad to hear that he would no longer be teaching us and that we would have to get used to a new one soon. It felt like something big was changing in my life, and I wasn't sure how to think of it at first.

But then, I began to think more positively about the situation; this could be good. This new teacher could bring his style of teaching, which could help me learn better than before. And maybe, he'll turn out to be even cooler than my old teacher was!

CREATIVE WRITING NUMBER 13

The boat

Example/Guide Answer

I remember my first time on a boat. I was excited to be out there, bobbing up and down on the waves. The sun was shining, the air was salty and fresh, and I couldn't help but feel alive! It felt like freedom in its purest form - no worries, just me and the open ocean.

Each journey after that only seemed to get better. Whether I was fishing, sailing or just enjoying a sunny day out at sea, nothing could compare to being on a boat. As soon as I stepped on board, all my troubles seemed to disappear as if by magic! It's like the waves' motion has calming powers that wash away stress and worries.

The boat is special to me; it has always comforted me when things weren't going well. The ship has been a part of my life for as long as I can remember.

When I was a small child, my dad would take me out on the boat every Saturday morning. We'd go fishing, and he'd tell me stories about his childhood adventures on the water. It was like stepping into another world when we were out there with just the wind and sea around us; it felt so peaceful and calming.

I learned how to navigate the boat with Dad's guidance, and soon enough, I became his co-captain! Together we explored all sorts of secret coves and winding rivers – some even had hidden waterfalls where we could go swimming! My love for boating grew from those early days, becoming integral to who I am. It's incredible to think that something so simple can bring so much joy to life.

CREATIVE WRITING NUMBER 14

The beach

Example/Guide Answer

The beach is my favourite place in the world. I love feeling the sand between my toes and listening to waves crashing in the distance. When I'm at the beach, it's like every worry and stress melts away. I love watching seagulls swooping by, dolphins splashing in the water and people sunbathing along the shoreline. It's so peaceful that I could stay there forever! The sound of children laughing and playing usually brings a smile to my face too!

One of my fondest memories was a family vacation when we all gathered on a nearby beach one summer day. We enjoyed lunch under an umbrella as ocean breezes cooled us off.

The ocean's breezes were so cool and calming; it felt like a dream. We had made sandwiches with our favourite ingredients and carefully packed them up along with some fruit and chips in a small picnic basket.

The sun shone brightly on us as we ate our lunch and talked about all sorts of things while watching people swimming in the water nearby. We even saw someone riding a surfboard! I laughed heartily at my friend's silly jokes as I nibbled away on my sandwich, feeling so content

CREATIVE WRITING NUMBER 15

The river

Example/Guide Answer

I remember the first time I saw a river. It was so grand and majestic, like something out of a dream. Every time I stepped closer, the sound of its rushing waters grew louder and more beautiful. The water sparkled in the sunlight as if it contained tiny diamonds, while the trees around it seemed to be whispering secrets to one another. I wanted nothing more than to lie beside it and stay there forever.

I have always been captivated by running rivers. The sound of their babbling, the rippling of the waves and its coolness on my bare skin; I love it.

As a child, nothing was more magical than exploring and playing alongside one of these living art pieces. I remember once when my friends and I went down to the river near our house. We got so carried away that we decided to go home at sunset!

We were having so much fun on the banks that soon enough, I wanted to lie down by the river and stay there forever. I felt like that place was my new home, a refuge from responsibilities, where I could relax in nature's goodness with no worries whatsoever.

The sound of rushing water filled my ears and echoed through my mind as if it were a song being sung to me. All around me was lush greenery that moved with every breeze, whispering with life and colour as far as my eye could see. At that moment, I knew there was no place in the world quite like this one, so special and unique that only this river could provide it to me.

CREATIVE WRITING NUMBER 16

The old house

Example/Guide Answer

I have fond memories of the old house. It was a large, two-storey house with a bright blue roof, surrounded by fields and trees in the countryside. As far back as I can remember, I was fascinated by the old house—it seemed like something out of a fairy tale. Every time we drove past it, I would crane my neck to get a better look at it.

Its wide windows sparkled in the sunlight, and its walls were whiter than snow. As I stepped closer, I could smell the faint scent of roses from deep within. It was as if this house was a living thing with stories to tell and secrets to keep - as if it wanted to let me in on them too.

I remember standing at that gate for ages, just staring at how grand but simple this house appeared. Now and again, a soft breeze would drift past and carry with its music from some faraway kingdom; it was mesmerising! My heart raced with anticipation whenever my gaze shifted away from those windows, almost expecting some magical creature or prince to come forward with open arms and invite me inside for tea.

The garden surrounding the house was full of beautiful flowers and plants that always bloomed, even during winter. It was full of butterflies and hummingbirds during summertime, and I remember watching them fluttering around the garden with wonderment. Going in through the front door felt like stepping into another world—it had high ceilings and big windows that let light pour into every room. It felt special, magical even, like no other place on earth.

CREATIVE WRITING NUMBER 17

The hotel

Example/Guide Answer

My first experience in a hotel was like a dream come true. I remember my mum and dad taking me to the hotel, and my eyes were wide open in awe of how grand it looked. I had never stayed at a hotel before, so when my family and I went on holiday, we decided to get a room. As soon as we stepped into the lobby, I was amazed. The beautiful architecture, grand staircases and artwork around the walls made me feel like royalty.

We went upstairs and opened the door to our room. It felt so special, with its comfy beds, luxurious furniture, and amazing view of the city outside. I immediately ran around the room, exploring every nook and corner.

I even had my own bathroom! The idea of having hot showers ready for me made me feel very pampered, almost like royalty! My parents laughed at how excited I was about all the amenities hotels provide. Still, they soon realised that this magical place would quickly become an essential part of our lives whenever we travel as a family.

The best part was that I could order room service whenever I wanted—calling down for food without worrying about cooking or cleaning up afterwards felt terrific. Everything was taken care of for me, making my stay much more enjoyable.

CREATIVE WRITING NUMBER 18

The balloon

Example/Guide Answer

The balloon is my favourite thing in the world. It gives me joy and excitement that I

can't get enough of. Whenever I see a brightly coloured balloon floating up into the sky, it immediately brings a smile. Watching the balloon slowly rises higher and higher until I can see a tiny dot in the distance always fills me with awe and wonder.

Every time I release a balloon, it's like magic! It never gets old; no matter how many times I witness it, each time holds something special. The sight of the balloon soaring ever higher until all I can see is a speck in the distance is truly breathtaking.

My imagination takes over as I think about where that little dot might be heading next. What kinds of places will it get to explore? Who will find it and wish upon its string? Does anyone else feel this same sense of wonder when watching this beautiful thing drift off like a butterfly?

No matter what answer lies ahead for my beloved balloon, nothing can lessen its beauty in my eyes.

CREATIVE WRITING NUMBER 19

The old man

Example/Guide Answer

As a child, I have always been drawn to old people. There's something almost magical about them; they often have an aura of wisdom and experience that enthrals me. One old man I remember is my neighbour, Mr Johnson. He was one of those larger-than-life characters who seemed to be born in the wrong era. He had a huge grey beard with twinkling blue eyes, always wore overalls and drove an antique truck that looked like it belonged in a museum.

Mr Johnson lived just down the street from me and was always kind and gentle. He had a beautiful garden that he worked on every day, tending to his flowers with love and care. Every morning, I'd see him in his garden reading the newspaper, no matter how cold outside.

He would always wave whenever we passed by, even when we were too busy to talk. During the summertime, he often shared some of his home-grown vegetables with us kids. Tomatoes were my favourite! Sometimes I'd stay after school to help him rake up leaves or shovel snow off the path leading to his house. In exchange for helping, he'd give me a few candies or tell me funny stories about his youth.

I used to love spending time with him as he'd tell me stories about his days at sea when he was younger or how things were "back in the day" - even though I wasn't alive then! Before returning home, he would take me for rides around town on Saturdays and buy me ice cream from our local ice-cream shop.

CREATIVE WRITING NUMBER 20

The accident

Example/Guide Answer

The accident happened so quickly that I can hardly remember the details. All I knew was that one second, everything was normal, and the next moment my world was turned upside down.

I had just gotten into my parents' car, and they drove me to school when it happened. We were stopped at a red light when a truck slammed into us from behind. It felt like an earthquake like our car was shaking around inside itself. My mum screamed, and my dad yelled something about seat belts as we spun off towards the side of the road.

I heard a loud bang and felt our car lurch forward, almost as if it were going to tip over. My heart stopped, and my stomach dropped as I realised what had happened.

I'm not sure how long it took for everything to settle, but eventually, we all came to a stop in a cloud of dust and smoke. Thankfully no one was hurt too badly, but we were all pretty shaken up from the whole experience.

CREATIVE WRITING NUMBER 21

The unfamiliar sound

Example/Guide Answer

The unfamiliar sound is so weird. I easily recognise familiar sounds like birds chirping and the neighbour's dog barking, but the unfamiliar sound throws me off guard. I'm never prepared for it because it's always something different. It could be a strange buzzing or a loud thump that makes me jump out of my seat.

When I heard an unfamiliar sound last week, I started running around, trying to figure out what was happening. It sounded like someone was banging on the door, but no one was there when I opened it. After searching every corner of my house, I finally realised that the noise came from a broken pipe in my basement. Thank goodness nothing else was wrong!

I still get anxious when I hear an unfamiliar sound, even though sometimes, they turn out to be harmless things like pipes or loose window shutters.

CREATIVE WRITING NUMBER 22

A weekend away

Example/Guide Answer

A weekend away is always an exciting adventure. I love to explore new places and try something different. A few months ago, I went on a special trip with my family, and it was one of the best weekends ever! We packed our car with all our essentials and set off on a long drive to the beach.

I can hardly contain my excitement as I help my parents pack the car for our beach trip. We carefully put in all our essentials, from beach towels and sand toys to snacks and plenty of water. I love watching my parents work together as a team to ensure we have everything we need for our adventure.

We finally buckled up and set off on our long drive to the beach. The sights along the way make me smile; it feels like an eternity before we arrive at the shoreline! With each mile, my anticipation grows more and more until I burst with joy at tasting the salty ocean air and feeling the sand between my toes.

The scenery was so beautiful as we drove along the coast, watching the waves crash against each shore. When we finally arrived at our destination, I couldn't believe how nice it was! Our hotel had a gorgeous ocean view, and it felt like paradise. We spent the day relaxing by the pool, playing games in the sand, and exploring nearby attractions. That night we enjoyed a delicious dinner together, followed by some stargazing under the starry sky - what an unforgettable experience.

The journey may be long, but every second is worth it when you're headed towards a dream destination like this one.

CREATIVE WRITING NUMBER 23

Moving house

Example/Guide Answer

Moving house is always an exciting time. Whenever I move, it feels like I'm starting all over again. New friends, new schools, and a new home - it's like an adventure! I love getting to know a new place and all the different things that come with it.

I love packing up all my things and imagining what the new house will look like. Every time we move, I can't help but feel excited about the new adventures that lie ahead. Will there be a bigger back garden where I can play with my friends? Or a treehouse for me to explore? The possibilities are endless, and they fill me with so much joy.

I like saying goodbye to familiar sights and sounds and creating a brand-new space in my new room when I get there. It's fun to pick out furniture and decorate it to reflect my personality. There's something special about making your own little corner of the world wherever you go - like you bring part of yourself with you no matter where life takes you!

Moving house is an experience that teaches me so much every time.

CREATIVE WRITING NUMBER 24

A family celebration

Example/Guide Answer

One of my favourite family celebrations is when we all celebrate my birthday. Everyone comes to our house, and it's always so much fun seeing them all. My mum prepares days in advance, baking a cake and making delicious food for everyone. We always have many decorations, balloons and streamers hanging from the ceiling and around the room.

I'm so excited to see everyone on the day that I can hardly contain myself. We start with a big dinner where everyone shares what they're thankful for about me. It's humbling to hear how proud they are of me, and their kind words fill me with warmth. After dinner, there's singing, dancing, and games until late into the night. Even though birthdays come every year, being surrounded by all my loved ones will never get old!

Afterwards, I get lots of presents from everyone, which is always exciting since I always need to figure out what I will get. Then it's time for cake and ice cream, so I can't help but smile when thinking about my birthday celebration. Everyone gets involved in helping me blow out the candles on my cake—it's the highlight of the evening. My siblings and cousins also love joining in on the festivities because they get to have fun too.

CREATIVE WRITING NUMBER 25

An event you remember from when you were young

Example/Guide Answer

When I was young, the most exciting event for me was when boys and girls in my neighbourhood got together for a big party. All of us were so happy to be able to join each other in games and activities. We raced around with each other, trying our best to see who could win first.

It felt like a celebration of summertime. Everyone was so happy to get out and play with each other after being cooped up inside all winter. We would have water balloon fights, play tag in the park, or just eat ice cream on someone's lawn while discussing our plans. Nothing compared to those days spent with my friends, enjoying this special time of year when we were so carefree and without any worries.

We split into teams of boys and girls, competing against each other in different challenges like running races or hiding and seeking. Not only did this give us all an opportunity to get along and interact with each other, but it also made the competition more interesting as we cheered on our own team! Whenever we had these events, it felt like we were one big family coming together to have fun, no matter how different our backgrounds were or how much older some of the kids were than others.

The most exciting part was seeing all the boys and girls together having fun! I remember looking around at everyone laughing, smiling and playing joyfully.

CREATIVE WRITING NUMBER 26

An animal attack

Example/Guide Answer

I still remember the day an animal attacked me. It was the scariest moment of my life! I had gone out on a walk in the woods and noticed a big, brown bear. The bear seemed to be getting closer and closer with each step. My fear began to rise higher and higher, yet somehow my feet kept moving faster and faster.

I knew there was no way to escape from this wild animal, but somehow, I was still running. It was like my body had taken over and refused to give up despite the fear that had overwhelmed me at that moment. Tears were streaming down my face as I heard the rustling sound of leaves coming from behind me; it sounded like the bear was still chasing me!

I didn't know how long I could keep running, but I refused to stop, even if it meant risking life or limb.

Fortunately, I managed to get away from the bear without getting hurt too badly. However, that experience made me realise just how unpredictable animals can be, even if they look not dangerous! Whenever I'm out in nature now, I stay alert and aware of my surroundings so that nothing like this ever happens again.

CREATIVE WRITING NUMBER 27

The school playground at night

Example/Guide Answer

The school playground at night is a mysterious place. It's full of shadows and strange noises that make it exciting, even though I'm a little scared. I like to go out there late at night when no one else is around and explore the darkness. It's like stepping into an alternate world. There are many things to discover, from the feel of the grass under my feet to the stars shining in the sky above me.

I love looking up and seeing so many stars at night--it's so much brighter than during the day! But what I love most about being in this special place when it's dark is that everything seems just a bit more magical than usual; it feels as if anything could happen at any moment. The playground is suddenly more inviting and inviting, even though nothing has changed since the last time I was there during the day.

I look around, and nothing has changed since the day before, yet something feels different. The swing set is calling my name, begging me to come and play on it. The slide looks even brighter; its colours catch the light in a way that makes me want to climb up and down it all day. Even the monkey bars seem lush with possibility as if they are ready for an adventure no matter how high I dare to go.

CREATIVE WRITING NUMBER 28

The lift pinged, and the door opened. I could not believe what was inside…

Example/Guide Answer

The lift pinged, and the door opened, revealing a sight that left me speechless. I couldn't believe my eyes as I stepped inside - it was like a dream come true! I had been expecting to step into an ordinary elevator but what lay before me was something out of this world - it felt like I'd stepped into one giant fairground! There were carnival rides, games, and food vans with mouth-watering treats everywhere around me. It was like being on cloud nine!

It was like being inside Aladdin's cave of delights. Everything I saw filled my heart with joy- there was something for everyone here. I felt like a kid in a candy store, unable to decide where to start exploring first.

I wanted to stay in that magical place forever, but unfortunately, my parents pulled me away so we could go back home. However, even though it was only for a moment, the experience left its mark on my heart, and I'll never forget it.

CREATIVE WRITING NUMBER 29

"Run!" he shouted as he thundered across the sand...

Example/Guide Answer

I vividly remember my dad's voice as he thundered across the beach. He was like a racehorse sprinting towards the finish line, except there was no race, and he never seemed to tire. I remember his laughter, full of joy, as we chased each other in circles around the beach. His deep baritone voice echoed out over the sand- "Run! Run!" he shouted with excitement.

I remember feeling like I was flying as I ran, sand kicking up behind me in a cloud. The sun was shining, and the ocean stretched out in front of us. I looked over my shoulder to see Daddy thundering right behind me, arms waving wildly above his head as he shouted. His voice filled the morning air and urged us to run faster. With that silly grin, he seemed so huge then, like nothing could beat him.

We kept running until we reached the sea, and when we did, Daddy scooped us both up under each arm and into the waves. We shrieked with delight at being thrown around by him, but he laughed it off - what did a bit of saltwater matter? After all, it was just more fun for us! We splashed around for hours, creating memories that would last forever

CREATIVE WRITING NUMBER 30

It was getting late as I dug in my pocket for the key to the door. "Hurry up!" she shouted from inside.

Example/Guide Answer

It was getting late, and I was feeling anxious. I had been outside for too long, playing with my friends, and the sun had started to set. As I slowly made my way home, I dug into my pocket for the key to the door. My fingers searched, but all they felt were loose coins and an old rock that reminded me of our visits to the beach last summer. I was in my own world, daydreaming about what I would be when I grew up. A firefighter? An astronaut? Anything seemed possible. But suddenly, everything changed!

I heard a voice coming from inside calling out for me - it was mom. "Hurry up!" she shouted as if she could read my mind, making me realise that time was running out.

I quickly searched in my pockets until finally; I found what had been missing -the key! Triumphantly holding it in front of me like a trophy, I ran towards the entrance, eager to get inside before anything else happened.

My mum stood there looking down at me with her arms crossed in front of her chest. Her face turned from frustration to amusement when she saw how dishevelled I looked from digging around for so long. She gently brushed away some dirt from my cheek that had come off from digging around with such fervour and smiled warmly before ushering me inside for dinner.

CREATIVE WRITING NUMBER 31

I know our back garden very well, but I was surprised at how different it looked at midnight...

Example/Guide Answer

I know my back garden like I know the back of my hand. Every inch of it is familiar, from the little bumps in the grass to the pattern on our patio stones. I thought nothing could surprise me about our garden--until one night when I stayed up past midnight and went out into it.

I slowly crept around the garden, taking time to appreciate its beauty in the moonlight. As opposed to during daytime when it looks like any ordinary backyard with patches of grass here and there, after midnight, it seemed almost magical.

The darkness gave everything an unfamiliar shape. The trees seemed taller than before, and shadows spread around them like tentacles reaching for me. Even though I knew all the plants in our back garden by name, each one looked different at night; their leaves glimmered white in the moonlight, giving them a magical feel.

But what surprised me was how quiet and still everything was once the sun had set. My backyard felt so peaceful without its usual buzz of life that it almost felt like I was on another planet.

CREATIVE WRITING NUMBER 32

Write a story using these 5 words: apple, train, elephant, paper and dog.

Example/Guide Answer

I was sitting in my room, eating an apple when I heard the loud sound of a train passing. It made me so excited that I immediately had the urge to go and explore it. So, I dropped my apple core and ran outside to see it. When the train went by, a huge white elephant was walking alongside it.

Even though elephants usually aren't seen here, this one looked majestic. I wanted to have something to remember this moment forever, so with trembling hands, I took out some paper and started sketching it. As I finished drawing it, a little black dog came running towards me with its tongue out! We smiled quickly before he bounded away again, playing with his friends.

The experience of watching the elephant and dog playing together while the train passed made me feel like life is full of beautiful surprises we don't always expect.

CREATIVE WRITING NUMBER 33

Digging down into the soft earth, the spade hit something metal…

Example/Guide Answer

Digging down into the soft earth, the spade hit something metal. My heart started beating faster as I carefully removed some of the dirt around it. I knew this could be a big moment for me, and my excitement was building with each shovelful of soil. I had been out here for hours already, searching for buried treasure in my backyard since I'd heard stories that pirates used to hide their loot around here ages ago. It seemed like all that waiting had been worth it; something under my feet. Really?

With my spade in hand, I had been digging for a few hours. The sun was setting, and I hadn't had any luck. I decided to go one last round and see if anything would turn up. As my spade dug deep into the soft earth, it hit something metal.

Excited, I started digging around the object to reveal what it was. To my surprise, it was an old chest filled with coins and jewellery! My heart raced as I uncovered each piece - colourful necklaces, shiny earrings, golden rings. It felt like a magical moment since all these things had been buried beneath the ground for so long; now, they were mine! It felt like a dream come true, and I couldn't believe that all this treasure belonged to me now.

CREATIVE WRITING NUMBER 34

Write a story which features the stopping of time.

Example/Guide Answer

I remember the daytime stopped like it was yesterday. I had been playing tag with a group of friends in the park, and we were having so much fun. Everyone was laughing and running around, completely unaware that something strange was about to happen.

Suddenly, we heard a loud noise, and everything froze in place. We were all standing still, unable to move or speak. We were all confused but also excited by this new experience. The birds stopped singing mid-note, and the wind stopped blowing. It felt like magic as if time had frozen us at this moment forever!

I'll never forget that amazement when I realised that time had stopped for us. Even though it only lasted for a few seconds, it made me appreciate those moments I spent with my friends even more than before.

CREATIVE WRITING NUMBER 35

Write a story which features an unusual method of transport.

Example/Guide Answer

My family and I had always wanted to go on a vacation together. Every summer, we would plan trips, but something always seemed to come up that prevented us from going anywhere. But this past summer, things changed! We decided to take a different approach and use an unusual method of transport- the hot air balloon!

We arrived at the launch site early in the morning, filled with excitement. The weather was perfect for a peaceful ride in the sky- not too windy or cloudy.

After all our preparations were done, we stepped into the basket of our balloon and waved goodbye as we took off. Up in the air, it felt like I was flying among the clouds. The silence was remarkable- no cars honking or people talking, just nature's music playing in my ears.

The view of my town was entirely different from high up in the clouds - like looking at a picture rather than real life. Every tree, every car and every house looked like a miniature version of itself. It was amazing to see my hometown from such an unusual perspective.

As we floated further away from our starting point, I noticed some animals flying alongside us in the same direction. Hot air balloons are also popular among birds who enjoy riding on its warm air currents.

CREATIVE WRITING NUMBER 36

The cry in the woods

Example/Guide Answer

The woods were always a special place for me. Whenever I was feeling down, I would take a walk in the woods and feel my troubles evaporate. Something so calming and peaceful about the dense trees and shrubbery made my worries melt away.

While walking in the woods one afternoon, I heard an eerie cry nearby. It sounded almost like a human voice crying out for help, yet it was distinctly animalistic. I stopped in my tracks and froze as fear coursed through me. After what felt like hours of standing still, the cry ceased abruptly, and all was silent once more.

It wasn't until later that I realised what had made that sound: it was probably a coyote howling at the moon. Knowing this calmed me considerably; the creature could have been miles away.

The cry in the woods has always fascinated me. It sounds so mysterious, like a long-forgotten secret wanting to be heard. I've heard it many times before, but no matter how much I listen, the mystery of it remains unsolved. My heart beats whenever I hear the cry, and I feel a chill down my spine. It's like something out of an old fairy tale or legend that nobody remembers anymore – yet there it is!

CREATIVE WRITING NUMBER 37

Write a story which features an escape

Example/Guide Answer

I was only seven years old when my parents, my two brothers, and I decided to take a family vacation. We were going on a grand adventure to an island far away, somewhere in the Caribbean. Everyone was so excited about our escape from reality for a week that we could barely contain ourselves. We had been planning the trip for months, and the time had finally come! I couldn't believe it. I remember my parents talking about all the fun activities we would do, like eating ice cream and going on boat rides every day. On the plane ride there, I felt like flying into an entirely new world filled with thrilling possibilities.

When we arrived at the beachy paradise of our destination island, it seemed almost too good to be true! The sun-kissed sand sparkled like diamonds, and the water was crystal clear and glistening in turquoise and blue. After spending days upon days exploring all sorts of nooks and crannies on the island, I knew this place would always hold a special place in my heart.

CREATIVE WRITING NUMBER 38

What do you want to be when you grow up and why?

Example/Guide Answer

As a child, I have always dreamed of becoming many different things when I grow up. From a veterinarian to a doctor, it's been difficult for me to settle on only one career. But recently, the answer has become clear- I want to be an engineer.

I've always been interested in how things work and how they can be improved upon. Engineering is the perfect way to combine my creativity and problem-solving skills into one rewarding profession that I find exciting. Also, it's never boring; engineers constantly have new challenges thrown their way.

Engineering allows me to help create solutions used in everyday life - from buildings, bridges and roads to machines or electronic devices!

CREATIVE WRITING NUMBER 39

If you could have any secret superpower, what would you want it to be and why?

Example/Guide Answer 39

I would have wanted to have the superpower of talking to animals. This superpower would be invaluable to me because it would allow me to get to know and understand different species in ways that were never possible. In my imagination, I can already see myself playing with a group of puppies and learning how they see the world. It's exciting to think of all the cute conversations we could have and the new friendships that would form.

With my animal communication power, I could communicate directly with cats, dogs, birds and any other creatures I came across. My conversations with them could allow me to gain knowledge of their thoughts and feelings by hearing their stories first-hand.

Furthermore, communicating with animals would make trips around the world super fun since I could visit any zoo or national park anywhere in the world and understand what each creature is saying when we meet.

CREATIVE WRITING NUMBER 40

Write about a time you felt happy. What happened? What made you feel happy?

Example/Guide Answer

I remember the time when I felt happy. It was during my birthday party when I was about 8 years old. All my friends were invited, and we played tag and hide-and-seek in the park. We also sang some of our favourite songs while eating delicious cupcakes. Everyone had a lot of fun, making me feel joyful and contented with my life.

Most importantly, all my family members were there too! My mum cooked some yummy food for us to enjoy, and my dad brought along his guitar to serenade us with his singing. Seeing everyone come together just for me made me feel incredibly special; it was a fantastic feeling that would stay with me forever. The love from everyone around me filled the air with a wonderful warmth I will always cherish.

CREATIVE WRITING NUMBER 41

If you were in charge of the whole world, what would you do to make the world a happier place?

Example/Guide Answer

If I were in charge of the whole world, I would ensure everyone had enough food to eat. No one should ever be hungry or go without a meal. I would also give everyone a place to call home so no one is left out in the cold. Everyone deserves a safe and warm place they can call their own.

Everyone should have nice places to live and enough money to buy things like toys, books, art supplies and clothes. No one should ever feel sad or alone when so many other people around could help them if we worked together better. That's why I want us all to learn how to share our thoughts without getting angry or upset with each other.

There should be no more hunger or people being sick because they can't afford what they need for their health.

CREATIVE WRITING NUMBER 42

Write a story about what it would be like to climb to the very top of Mt. Everest.

Example/Guide Answer

Climbing Mt. Everest has been my dream since I was young. Reaching the peak of the highest mountain in the world would be a fantastic accomplishment and one I've wanted to do for as long as I can remember. The thought of standing at the very top fills me with excitement.

The journey to get there would be challenging, but climbing Mt. Everest is something that will make me even stronger than before. Even though there may be tough moments throughout my climb, each step will bring me closer to achieving my goal and makes it worth it in the end. With every bit of strength and determination, I'm confident I can make it to the top!

Climbing to the very top of Mt. Everest would be an incredible adventure! It would take a long time and a lot of hard work. The trek up the mountain would be filled with breathtaking views, chilly air, and lots of snow! Of course, there would be challenges, too, like tricky terrain and unpredictable weather. But when I finally make it to the top, it will all be worth it.

The view from such a high-up must feel like standing on top of the world. How amazing that must look - seeing everything around you and knowing that you made it to one of the highest points on Earth.

CREATIVE WRITING NUMBER 43

If you were in charge of planning the school lunch menu, what foods would you serve each day?

Example/Guide Answer

If I were in charge of planning the school lunch menu, I would make sure to serve nutritious meals that are also tasty and fun!

On Mondays, I would prepare a hearty soup with some fresh-baked bread.

Tuesdays would be all about tacos: hard shells taco shells filled with refried beans and shredded cheese.

Wednesdays would be for sandwiches – turkey on wheat or peanut butter and jam sandwiches.

Thursdays, it's time for pizza – classic pepperoni or maybe something more adventurous like buffalo chicken?

Fridays are always fun, so I'd make mac & cheese with broccoli florets mixed in – yum! Also, a side of salad and some freshly cut fruit.

CREATIVE WRITING NUMBER 44

Imagine that dogs take over the world. What do they make the humans do?

Example/Guide Answer

Imagine a world where dogs take over the reins and humans become their subservient race. The dogs would make us do all sorts of things to satisfy their interests. We'd be forced to feed them fancy snacks and take them on long walks.

It would be the best thing if dogs took over the world! Their new canine overlords would make humans do all kinds of things.

Not only that, but we'd also have to give up our beds for the doggies' comfort. That's right - no more sleeping in for us humans! Instead, we'd have to wake up early each morning just like we used to, but this time it's not for work or school – it's solely devoted to ensuring our canine overlords are well taken care of.

We'd be required to pet the pups and play with them as much as possible.

CREATIVE WRITING NUMBER 45

Write a story about flying to outer space and discovering a new planet.

Example/Guide Answer

I had always dreamed of flying to outer space and discovering a new planet. I was ecstatic when I finally got the chance; my spaceship was ready, and I could feel myself getting closer to achieving my dream.

When I left Earth's atmosphere, it felt like nothing else mattered; all my worries were gone as soon as I entered the vastness of space. The stars twinkled in the distance, creating an enchanted environment for exploration. As I journeyed farther away from home, exciting possibilities revealed themselves—a new planet tucked away in a distant corner of the universe just waiting to be discovered!

Finally, after a long voyage, I spotted something that caught my eye: an unfamiliar celestial body surrounded by asteroids and comets that glowed with mysterious energy. This must be the planet that I'd been hoping to find. As I explore this brand-new world, every step forward leads to something even more exciting than before.

CREATIVE WRITING NUMBER 46

Describe what it is like when trees lose all their leaves in the autumn season.

Example/Guide Answer

When autumn comes around, I always look forward to the leaves changing colour. The shades of red and orange look like a painting in the sky. But even more exciting is when all the leaves finally fall off the trees. It's almost like the trees are getting ready for a nap because they will be bare for so long.

The autumn season is a magical time of year. When the leaves start to change colour, I know it's time for the trees to shed their summer clothes and prepare for winter. Seeing all the vibrant oranges, reds, and yellows on the trees can be breathtaking. As November approaches, all those beautiful colours slowly disappear as the chilly winds blow them away.

It saddens me to see all the trees losing their leaves, but then I remember that they need this rest to survive during the colder months. Once they have lost all their leaves, it's like they take a big nap until springtime, when everything will be green again. Nature is giving us a special goodbye before we enter winter.

It's quiet, too; there's no rustling of leaves on windy days, only empty branches swaying without them. I love how everything looks different; every street and park has been transformed into an entirely new place. Walking through my neighbourhood feels completely different, with no leaves on the ground or trees above me. Even though it feels strange, I still find it peaceful and beautiful in its own way.

CREATIVE WRITING NUMBER 47

Imagine what it might be like to live on a boat

Example/Guide Answer

Living on a boat would be a fantastic experience. I think about what it would be like to wake up every morning and look out the window to see nothing but blue waters. It would also be fun to sail around to different places, see new sights and meet new people. I could learn many skills like tying knots and navigation that you don't find in everyday life.

I can imagine waking up to waves gently rocking me back and forth. There is nothing but blue sky, bright sun, and deep water everywhere I look. There would be plenty of time for swimming, fishing, and exploring new beaches and towns. On the deck, I could sunbathe or watch dolphins playing in the distance.

And every night, we could anchor somewhere special and fall asleep under a blanket of stars. Waking up early to watch the sunrise over a beautiful landscape each day; sounds like paradise. Taking part in activities such as swimming, fishing or experiencing first-hand what it's like to live off-grid while enjoying some time away from technology would make this adventure even more memorable.

Living on a boat is something exciting; you're always on an adventure! Every day could bring something new - from discovering a hidden cove to battling rough weather conditions - it would be an unforgettable experience. Of course, it wouldn't hurt to learn all about sailing!

CREATIVE WRITING NUMBER 48

If you had one wish, what would it be?

Example/Guide Answer

If I had one wish, it would be to have the ability to fly. I remember running outside and using my imagination to pretend I could fly. It would be so cool to soar above the clouds and feel the wind in my hair. Imagine the view from up there, seeing everything below me! I could go anywhere without worrying about taking a car or hopping on an aeroplane. I'd also love being able to experience all the different kinds of weather that come with flying around - like feeling a stormy rain shower or watching as snow falls from above.

I'd even use my new power for fun things too. I was taking a midnight flight over my city or doing some awesome tricks in the sky, like dives and flips! Imagine how much faster I'd get places - no more traffic jams or missed buses. From a young age, this has been my one wish, something unique for me that nobody else has or can experience ever again.

CREATIVE WRITING NUMBER 49

Write about what you might do if you have the superpower to become invisible.

Example/Guide Answer

The possibilities would be endless If I had the superpower to become invisible. I could visit all my favourite places without anyone noticing me. I could sneak into movie theatres for free or climb tall buildings and explore their roofs. With my invisibility power, I could go anywhere and do anything.

I could sneak into places that aren't usually accessible and explore them without anybody noticing. I would love to visit the White House or Buckingham

Palace and explore their secret passageways. That would be such an adventure!

Imagine being able to hide in a friend's room without them even knowing! It would be so much fun sneaking around, pulling funny stunts and making an epic mess they'd have to clean up afterwards. I would also use my special powers sparingly so that it could be more exciting - like playing hide-and-seek with my friends or surprising them when they least expect it.

I could also use my power of invisibility to help people in need by going undercover and getting information. For instance, if anyone was missing, I could use my powers to investigate further and find out who took them or where they are hiding. By being invisible, no one will know it's me doing the detective work, so that might make it easier for me to get all the information needed.

CREATIVE WRITING NUMBER 50

Imagine you've invented the time machine! What year do you travel to and why?

Example/Guide Answer

If I had invented the time machine, my first destination would be 2040! I'm sure it will be a great experience. I want to see what kind of technology and inventions have been made by then. They may even have a teleportation machine by then. It would be so cool to travel around the world in an instant. But if not, they may have a flying car that could take me wherever I want.

Exploring this futuristic world and seeing all its cool inventions would be so much fun. I'd even speak the language they were using back then - if it's different from what we have now! Also, I could find out if any new types of candy or food are being made. That would be such an exciting adventure!

I also can't wait to learn what new clothes people wear and how different the fashion trends are compared to today's styles. They may have figured out how to make all their clothes from recycled materials. That would be awesome! And hopefully, there won't be any wars or discrimination either.

CREATIVE WRITING NUMBER 51

What is a food you hate? Describe it

Example/Guide Answer

I hate mushrooms. They have a slimy texture and are squishy; it's like eating goo. The taste isn't the best either; it has an almost bitter flavour that I can't stand. Every time I see a mushroom on my plate, my stomach turns. Not only do they look disgusting to me, but their smell is also unpleasant and makes me want to gag. Whenever my family orders pizza, I always ask for extra cheese instead of mushrooms because there's no way I'm putting that disgusting fungus in my mouth.

Mushrooms remind me of something you'd find if you were walking through the forest, which is so not appetising. They look so alien-like with their dark brown-ish caps and white stems that it's creepy. No, thank you! I'll take fries or a bowl of ice cream over mushrooms any day. Yuck!

My least favourite thing about mushrooms is when they're cooked in a sauce or with other ingredients. Even if the food looks appetizing, it takes away all my appetite and ruins the meal for me as soon as I spot them. When this happens, all the hard work that goes into making the dish is wasted on someone who won't even eat it!

CREATIVE WRITING NUMBER 52

Write a story about being the ruler of an underwater world.

Example/Guide Answer

My name is King Cosmo, and I am the ruler of an underwater world. The sea creatures love me because I look after them and ensure they are safe from danger. Every morning I swim around my kingdom to check on my loyal subjects. Exploring the ocean's depth and discovering something new every day is so much fun.

I have so many exciting adventures in my underwater world! Sometimes I go on an epic journey with some dolphins or challenge a giant octopus to a race! One time, we even had a big party with all kinds of colourful fish swimming around us while we ate jellyfish snacks and played music made by clams.

Creating wonderful memories with these fantastic creatures living in my kingdom is incredible.

CREATIVE WRITING NUMBER 53

If you could be any animal, which one would you be and why?

Example/Guide Answer

If I could be any animal, it would have to be a butterfly. Fluttering from flower to flower, the thought of being able to fly freely and gracefully around the world is captivating! I love how delicate and beautiful butterflies are - with their bright colours and intricate patterns. It's like they were made for beauty itself.

I've always thought that butterflies are beautiful and that they can fly, which is a bonus. Being able to soar in the sky and look down on the world below would be amazing. All their colours make them look like little pieces of art. It's no wonder why people think they are so special.

I also love how butterflies symbolise transformation and new beginnings; it'd be cool to represent that kind of message as an animal. No matter what situation you're in, you can always find beauty and hope when it comes to starting anew. Who wouldn't want to flutter around with their colourful wings? Flying sounds like a lot of fun too!

CREATIVE WRITING NUMBER 54

Have you ever forgotten to do your homework? What happened?

Example/Guide Answer

I remember it like it was yesterday. The moment I realised that I had forgotten to do my homework for the next day. It was a Monday, and usually, on Mondays, homework was due for the week. But here I was, realising that my hard work and dedication would not be rewarded because of my absent-mindedness.

I hastily looked through all my notebooks, frantically searching for anything related to the assignment, but nothing. I became frustrated with myself, feeling like a complete failure because of this mistake.

How could I have let this happen? My mind raced with thoughts; what would happen when I told my teacher that I didn't do the homework? What will they think of me? All these worries grew into one big mess inside me as I tried to figure out what to do next.

CREATIVE WRITING NUMBER 55

Do you like theme parks? What are some of your favourite rides?

Example/Guide Answer

I love theme parks! I'm always so excited to go, and my parents know that it's one of my favourite things to do. I even like standing in line for the rides because there's always time to chat with my family and friends.

My favourite ride is the roller coaster. Nothing compares to feeling a huge

adrenaline rush when you drop down from the highest point, and your stomach feels like it is floating! I also love spinning rides like the teacups because they make me dizzy in all the best ways. The Ferris wheel is my favourite ride, though - it makes me feel like I am on top of the world, looking down on everything around me.

I also enjoy other rides, such as log flumes and carousels. Going around in circles on the carousel never gets old; I love how calming it can be. And when it comes to log flumes, it's almost like you're getting two rides in one--the anticipation for the first drop is thrilling before you even get splashed with water!

There's just something so calming about soaring above everyone else while enjoying a peaceful view of all below.

CREATIVE WRITING NUMBER 56

Write a story using these three words: detective, piano, and pizza.

Example/Guide Answer

I'm a detective, but not your ordinary kind. My detective work involves finding lost objects. One case was strange and yet exciting. I had been called in to investigate the missing pizza from one family's dinner table.

My first clue was a piano, which seemed like an odd hint. I glanced around the room and noticed that it was filled with music sheets scattered everywhere. It didn't take long for me to deduce that this family liked their pizza as much as they enjoyed their music! So, I started my investigation by following the sound of notes playing from the piano's keys.

I eventually tracked down the lost pizza in an old, abandoned building down the street! It turns out that someone hadn't finished their dinner, so they decided to take it with them on their way back home after playing some tunes on the piano.

CREATIVE WRITING NUMBER 57

Is there a homework subject you dread? Why do you not like getting homework in that subject?

Example/Guide Answer

I hate getting homework in mathematics. Maths is difficult because I'm not the best at numbers and equations. No matter how often my teacher tries to explain it to me, I still can't seem to get it right. Math is probably my least favourite subject, and when I get assigned a difficult problem, I just want to curl up in a ball and cry. The teacher doesn't even care that it's so hard for me! Why can't they assign us easier problems that are fun?

Whenever I get a question wrong on tests or quizzes, I feel like giving up because I don't understand why the answers are what they are. And then, after spending hours doing maths homework that I don't understand, all my hard work goes down the drain when I get other bad marks in the class.

Maths is one of those subjects where you need to think logically and solve puzzles quickly - something that doesn't come naturally to me. The worst part about maths homework is that it takes forever to finish one problem, let alone an entire assignment! Every time I try something new, I need clarification and must start over again. My friends who understand math make it look super easy, but something works out differently whenever I try to do it myself! It almost makes me not want even to bother trying at all.

CREATIVE WRITING NUMBER 58

What are you grateful for today and why?

Example/Guide Answer

Today, I am so grateful for my family and friends. They are always there to make me laugh, even when I don't feel like it. My mum is the most amazing cook in the world, and she ensures that I never go hungry. She also helps me with my homework and encourages me to follow my dreams. My dad is super funny; he always cracks a joke or two! He also supports everything I do and gives good advice whenever needed.

I'm thankful for all the close friends that I have too! Whether we're studying at school or hanging out together, they always make sure that I'm having fun. They understand all my jokes and share the same interests as me. We've been through a lot together, so it's nice to have someone who gets what you're going through.

Finally, I'm thankful for the fun activities I experience as a kid. Whether playing street hockey on the weekend or camping with my family during the summer, these experiences give me something new to look forward to each week. It's incredible how much joy and excitement can bring, no matter what age you are!

CREATIVE WRITING NUMBER 59

Write a story about a snowy day.

Example/Guide Answer

The morning of the snow day began like any other, with the sun rising and the birds singing melodic tunes. I awoke to a gentle sound different from my usual alarm clock - soft, fluffy snowflakes falling on our rooftop. My eyes lit up, seeing all the white powder falling from the sky. I quickly jumped out of bed, put on my warmest winter clothes, and ran outside to make snow angels and build a giant igloo.

My arms moved quickly as I tried to form an angel shape in the snow, but the crisp powder kept falling back onto me. With every move I made, more white flakes flew around me in a flurry until there were no more left.

My friends soon joined me as we created a snowball battle line in our backyard. Snowballs were being thrown left and right as laughter echoed throughout our neighbourhood. It was such a fantastic feeling! We spent hours outside making memories that would last us a lifetime before finally retreating inside for some hot cocoa by the fireplace.

CREATIVE WRITING NUMBER 60

Currently, it is required by law that kids go to school. Do you think this is a good or bad idea?

Example/Guide Answer

It is a great idea for kids to be required to go to school by law. It allows us to learn about the world and all its wonders. A school is a place where we can develop our knowledge, skills, and talents. With education, we can gain confidence in ourselves and discover new interests or passions that will help us in our futures.

Not only is going to school beneficial academically but also socially. In school, we get the chance to make new friends and learn how to interact with different kinds of people in a safe environment. We also get access to plenty of extracurricular activities and clubs, which give us even more chances for socialisation.

Overall, I believe it's an excellent idea for kids like me who are eager and excited about learning.

CREATIVE WRITING NUMBER 61

What are things you learned today?

Example/Guide Answer

Today I learned something cool! I was playing around with my toys when my dad told me that a day is longer than 24 hours. He said it's closer to 24 hours and 30 minutes, so we almost get an extra hour every day. I was so excited that I ran around the house shouting about it.

I also learned something interesting about the moon. My dad explained that the moon takes 28 days to orbit around Earth, which is why we have a full moon once a month. It was amazing to learn how our planet relates to the moon and how they orbit each other in perfect harmony. He showed me some pictures of what it looks like from outer space, which was fantastic.

My parents always found fun ways to teach me new things, and today was no exception.

CREATIVE WRITING NUMBER 62

Would you rather have a goldfish or shark as a pet? Why?

Example/Guide Answer

If I could have any pet, it would be a goldfish! Goldfish are so fun to watch as they swim around and explore their tank. Plus, they come in all different colours, making it easy to find one that matches my style. They don't require too much work, just food and occasional tank maintenance, so I won't need to stress out over keeping them alive. Also, goldfish can live for several years, so I get to make a long-term commitment with my new friend!

On the other hand, sharks are very cool animals, but not something I would want as a pet. They look powerful and ferocious in movies, but most shark species need large open ocean environments with plenty of room to move around.

CREATIVE WRITING NUMBER 63

What are 3 things you can do that are good for the environment?

Example/Guide Answer

As a kid, I have had the opportunity to learn about how my small everyday behaviours can help create a healthier and safer environment. It is important that I do what I can to contribute positively. Three things that are good for the environment are: recycling, conserving water, and using reusable containers when possible.

Recycling is an easy habit for me to practice as it requires very little effort. Making sure that any plastic bottles or cans go into the recycling bin instead of the trash makes a difference in reducing waste. Additionally, not throwing away paper helps reduce the need for cutting down trees and encourages more sustainable practices within our communities.

I also conserve water whenever possible by taking shorter showers and turning off the tap when brushing my teeth or washing dishes.

CREATIVE WRITING NUMBER 64

What did you do during the summer holiday last year? What do you want to do for the summer holiday this year?

Example/Guide Answer

It was so much fun last year when my family and I went on a summer holiday. We took a drive to the beach, which was exciting. We got to build sand-castles in the sand and go swimming in the ocean. My brother and I even caught some fish off our boat. Enjoying time outdoors with my family and exploring new places was incredible. Spending time outdoors with my family is one of the best feelings I could ever experience.

Last summer was so much fun! I hope that this summer we can do something just as fun as last year's adventure. This time, I want to go camping. It would be cool to learn how to start a campfire and roast marshmallows by it. If there are nearby lakes, we can also try fishing again as we did at the beach. That might be a lot of fun too.

I'm hoping that this summer, we can have an even bigger adventure than last time. This time, instead of staying in one place each week, we can try different activities while travelling from one place to another. That way, we experience many other things and make wonderful memories together. It will be just as fun as last year's journey.

CREATIVE WRITING NUMBER 65

Write a story about a superhero dog who saves the day! Who does the dog help and why?

Example/Guide Answer

Once upon a time, there was an adorable puppy with superpowers! His name was Super-Pup, and he had the unique ability to fly. He was a brave pup who wanted to use his powers to help others in need. One day, while flying around town, Super-Pup saw a family of ducks stuck in a tree! They were too scared to jump down and kept quacking for help. Super-Pup flew up into the tree with his super strength and gently lifted each duckling back onto the ground until they were all safe.

. . .

THE FAMILY of ducks thanked Super-Pup with lots of wet puppy kisses before hopping off into the pond nearby. But that wasn't all—Super Pup still had another adventure ahead.

Super-Pup is my superhero!

CREATIVE WRITING NUMBER 66

What does the word courage mean to you?

Example/Guide Answer

Courage was something that I had to learn more about. It meant being brave in the face of danger, like when my big brother would go exploring deep into the woods and come back with stories of his adventures.

He taught me that courage isn't just about facing physical threats-- it's also about having the strength to do the right thing even when you're scared or not sure how you should act. I remember that feeling when I stood up for a friend at school who a group of other kids was bullying- standing up to them felt scary but doing what was right made me proud.

Courage is something that is within us all, no matter our age or experience; it means having faith in yourself and believing you can make a positive difference in your life and the lives of others.

CREATIVE WRITING NUMBER 67

Write an essay that starts with the line, "Tomorrow, I hope…"

Example/Guide Answer

Tomorrow, I hope to have some extra time for myself. A time that I don't need to use for homework or chores. It would be a special treat that I can use however I wish. I'll take a walk and explore the neighbourhood, checking out all the plants and animals nearby. There must be so many things in my backyard that I have yet to notice! Even if it's just an hour or two, it will allow me to step away from schoolwork and relax with nature.

I also hope tomorrow brings an opportunity to learn something new - a craft project my mother has been teaching me or another language we've been studying together. Whenever I'm learning something new, my brain works its hardest!

CREATIVE WRITING NUMBER 68

If you had a tree that grows money, what would you do?

Example/Guide Answer

If I had a tree that grows money, I would be in my wildest dreams! All the wonderful things I could do with all those coins and notes. Imagine how much fun it would be to have such a fantastic tree if only it were possible. Just imagine being able to pick coins and banknotes off the branches like apples. Every day could be a treasure hunt as I rummage through the leaves and find whatever surprises await me. It would make life so much more exciting.

I would use some money to buy more toys for myself and my friends. We could go shopping together and get whatever we wanted without worrying about the cost or our parents telling us no. Going out to eat at fancy places and getting ice cream whenever we wanted to - there'd be no stopping us!

What I'd love most, though, is sharing with my family and friends.

CREATIVE WRITING NUMBER 69

What are some safety tips you should follow when riding a bike?

Example/Guide Answer

Riding a bike can be a fun and exciting activity but staying safe is important. Here are some safety tips you should follow when going for a ride.

First off, make sure you always wear a helmet. Wearing a helmet can help protect your head from injury in the case of an accident or fall.

It also helps to wear bright colours so drivers can easily see you on the road. Try to stick to bike paths or well-lit roads that have less traffic and are easier to navigate.

It's essential to pay attention while riding; you must stay alert and watch out for obstacles like potholes or rocks in the path ahead.

CREATIVE WRITING NUMBER 70

Are you afraid of the dark? Why or why not?

Example/Guide Answer

The dark can be a very scary thing to me. I get scared of all sorts of things when it's nighttime, and the lights are off. I worry that there might be monsters hiding in the dark corners or that something might reach out and grab me from under my bed. It's like an eerie feeling takes over my body and fills me with fear.

My parents try their best to make me feel safe, but no matter what they do, it doesn't always work. Sometimes I will bring a torch into my room, so I don't have to worry about anything hiding in the shadows. Other times, I'll ask them to stay with me until I fall asleep so I'm not alone in the darkness. No matter what, it still feels intimidating being surrounded by nothing but blackness while lying in bed at night.

I sometimes get so scared at night that I keep my bedroom light on until morning. Even then, sometimes, I find myself sitting in bed shaking because I am afraid of the darkness around me.

CREATIVE WRITING NUMBER 71

Write a superhero story where the villain wants to become good.

Example/Guide Answer

Once upon a time, a villain wanted to become good. He had been naughty since birth and didn't know the difference between right and wrong. But one day, he realised that if he kept being bad, no one would want to be his friend, so he decided to try to turn over a new leaf.

He started by doing small things like helping old ladies cross the street and returning money that people dropped. Soon enough, word spread about this mysterious "saviour", as some called him, who was trying to change his ways. Everyone in the town became fascinated with him and wanted to get to know him better, even though they feared him at first.

It wasn't easy for this former villain-turned-hero, but eventually, everyone accepted him as one of their own. It was a long, hard road for this former villain-turned-hero. Everyone knew that he had been a horrible person for a long time. He had caused trouble and hurt others, so nobody wanted anything to do with him. But then he decided to change and become a hero instead of an evildoer. He worked hard, learning to use his powers for good instead of evil. And over time, people started to notice his changes and began giving him a chance they had never done before.

Slowly but surely, one by one, people began accepting this new hero as their own. They saw how much effort he put into making things right again and were impressed by his dedication. Eventually, even those who hadn't believed in him at first were won over by his commitment and transformation from villain to hero.

CREATIVE WRITING NUMBER 72

Describe your dream bedroom. What would be in it and why?

Example/Guide Answer

My dream bedroom would be filled with lots of fun things. Every morning I would wake up to find all my favourite stuffed animals, like teddy bears and unicorns, scattered around my room. I'd have bright pink walls, so everything in the room looked cheerful and colourful. I would also have a white canopy bed with fluffy pillows and a cosy blanket. There would be a giant closet where I could store all my clothes, toys, and games.

I'd have a desk in the corner of the room where I could draw pictures or work on puzzles. To finish off my dream bedroom, it would include some fun decorations like wall stickers, sparkly lights and curtains that matched the bright pink walls. One of my favourite things about this room is that it has enough space for me to play with all my toys without making a mess.

I love inviting friends around, too, so we can have lots of fun playing together. It's great to show off my collection - especially when new friends come over. When I've had enough of the toys, there's still enough space in my room for reading books or doing art projects. I always feel calm and content when spending time here; it is like a mini paradise.

CREATIVE WRITING NUMBER 73

You get £100 but you have to spend it by the end of the day. What do you do with it?

Example/Guide Answer

If I had £100 to spend by the end of the day, I would have so much fun! First, I'd buy something yummy, like ice cream or a big pizza. Maybe I'd even invite my friends over and split it with them.

After that, I'd go shopping for cool toys and clothes. There are so many things that are just begging me to buy them. Who could resist?

Then, if there's any money left over, I'll put it in my piggy bank. That way, I can save up for something special next time. Having £100 all to myself is like a dream come true - having the chance to do whatever I want makes it even better.

Being able to buy things I want and save up for something special will be so awesome. I'm even going to get to donate some of it if I choose to! It feels so amazing knowing that this money is my own and that no one else can tell me what I should do with it.

I'm already thinking about how much fun this money could help me have - my friends and I will be able to go out for pizza or watch movies together when we hang out. And since it's mine, there won't be any fighting over who pays what, either! Having £100 all to myself makes me feel like a grown-up, but in the best way possible.

CREATIVE WRITING NUMBER 74

You're trapped on a desert island with only the things in your schoolbag. What do you do?

Example/Guide Answer

As a kid stuck on a desert island with only the things in my schoolbag, I was filled with terror and despair. What would I do? How would I survive? Then, out of the corner of my eye, I saw some coconuts on nearby palm trees. The fear disappeared and was replaced by excitement as I realised that having access to food could help me survive here.

Suddenly, being stuck here seems alright. First things first, I need to figure out how to survive. Luckily, plenty in my bag can help me do just that.

My pencil case is full of pens and highlighters that can be used as kindling for a fire; luckily enough, my maths textbook is made of paper, so it will also make a great fuel. With these things at hand, I've got all the resources to make a nice campfire and cook food.

Then, I decided to explore what else the area had to offer and soon discovered some fish swimming in a nearby pond. Then it hit me; this deserted island might be fun! Possibilities were suddenly everywhere, and ideas popped into my head faster than anything before building a raft, finding shelter, and making fire; all these activities kept me busy for days.

CREATIVE WRITING NUMBER 75

You are an inventor whose job is to create the best toys. What will you make?

Example/Guide Answer

As an inventor of toys, my job is to bring joy and happiness to children all around the world. I'll create the best and most imaginative toys ever to accomplish this. My first invention will be a life-size robotic dog that can interact with kids in a fun and friendly manner. This robot pup will come with different voices, colours, and expressions so it can truly feel like one's own furry friend. It's sure to be a hit!

Next will be an interactive board game combining virtual reality technology with traditional board game pieces. Kids will explore fun new environments while competing against their friends or siblings for the highest score. The game pieces can take on any form imaginable, from cute animals and magical creatures to robots and aliens - whatever takes their fancy!

I would also invent a robotic dinosaur that sings songs and dances when you press its back. It also has four different game modes, so there will always be something new for kids to explore.

CREATIVE WRITING NUMBER 76

Your pet is in charge of you for a day. What will they make you do?

Example/Guide Answer

If my pet were in charge of me for a day, it would be so much fun! My pet is a Labrador Retriever named Spot. He loves to run and play games, so I can imagine what kind of things he would have me do during our time together.

First, I'm sure he'd want to go on a long walk around the neighbourhood and sniff all his favourite spots. Then, we could go to the park and play Frisbee or catch until we were both exhausted.

Finally, I bet he'd want us to cuddle up on the couch with some treats for a quiet movie night.

No matter what Spot has planned for us that day, it will be an adventure! We'll make many memories while doing all kinds of silly activities together.

CREATIVE WRITING NUMBER 77

When I discovered there was treasure buried in the backyard I…

Example/Guide Answer

When I discovered there was treasure buried in the backyard, I couldn't believe my eyes. It felt like a dream come true! I had heard stories of hidden pirates' gold and sunken gems, but nothing had prepared me for such an exciting find.

As I dug through the dirt and pebbles with my shovel, my heart raced in anticipation of what might be hidden beneath the surface. Suddenly, something sparkly caught my eye, and when I brushed away some soil, to my absolute delight, it was a real coin.

After that first discovery, all bets were off - it was like a race against time as each clump of soil revealed more treasure. Every swipe of the shovel brought forth some new item from another time, making me feel like an archaeologist uncovering ancient artefacts.

CREATIVE WRITING NUMBER 78

The moment I woke up, I knew something wasn't right…

Example/Guide Answer

The moment I woke up, I knew something wasn't right. My room was brighter than usual, and the sunlight was coming from all directions. I looked out of my window to see that the sky was a deep shade of pink and orange - something completely unnatural. As I slowly got out of bed, the room began to hum with an unfamiliar noise that filled me with a dread.

I glanced around nervously and noticed that everything in my bedroom had been rearranged in strange patterns; furniture pieces were stacked in precarious piles, toys had been arranged on top of dressers, and books were scattered across the floor. It almost felt like someone had come into my room while I was sleeping! All these strange changes made me scared and confused about what could be happening outside my door - what other bizarre occurrences did this new day hold?

As I stepped into the hallway, I couldn't help but feel a chill go down my spine. Everywhere I looked, something seemed to be off. As if everything had been replaced overnight with strange new things that didn't look right. Every object had an eerie quality about it, and nothing felt normal anymore.

CREATIVE WRITING NUMBER 79

Write about the best magic trick you can imagine.

Example/Guide Answer

Ever since I was a young child, I have been fascinated by the idea of magic. Whenever I saw a magic trick performed on stage, I couldn't help but wonder what it would be like to do it myself. So, when I was finally given a chance to try one out for myself, that's exactly what I did.

I dreamed of being a master magician. I imagined myself performing the most spectacular and mysterious tricks that would surprise my audience. But one trick that truly captivated me was the idea of making an elephant disappear. This trick seemed so far-fetched and impossible, yet part of me believed it could be achieved with enough practice and determination.

I loved to imagine how I could make this magic trick come alive, picturing myself on stage with an elephant standing beside me and pointing at it as my audience watched in awe. With a wave of my hand, I'd pull off the most epic disappearing act ever seen! The possibilities were endless: would the elephant vanish into thin air? Would he disappear right before their eyes? It filled my childhood fantasies with magical delights.

CREATIVE WRITING NUMBER 80

Describe a day in your life if you were famous kid.

Example/Guide Answer

Every day would be a whirlwind of excitement. If I were a famous kid, I'd get up early in the morning to greet the paparazzi outside my house and take some pictures. Then it would be off to school, where I'd have fans waiting for autographs and photographers clamouring for more photos.

Even in class, I couldn't escape the attention as people tried to sneak their way into the room to catch a glimpse of me. After school, there would be interviews with various TV shows, magazines and websites to promote whatever project I was working on.

Finally, at night when all was said and done, I'd head home with an entourage of friends who had been invited over by fans to hang out together and do something fun.

CREATIVE WRITING NUMBER 81

You discover an island no one has ever seen before. Describe what it's like.

Example/Guide Answer

Walking along the beach, I stumbled upon something strange and mysterious. It was an island entirely new to me, with lush green grass and trees swaying in the wind. What a fantastic discovery. I knew I had to explore it further and see what this place was about.

Climbing over the rocky shore and through a small forest of palm trees, I came across a clearing with a mountain in the middle of it. Atop this mountain, vast flowers bloom in vibrant colours, including yellow daisies, purple dahlias, and white lilies. There were also plenty of animals everywhere, from birds chirping high up in the tree branches to fish swimming in the crystal-clear ocean below.

Every moment felt like an adventure for the first time in my life! Every road led to an exciting discovery, from a vibrant beach full of life to a magnificent mountain peak stretching towards the sky. Even simple things like watching a caterpillar slowly make its way across a leaf or smelling wildflowers' sweet aroma opened new perspectives for me. It was magical.

CREATIVE WRITING NUMBER 82

I looked out the window and couldn't believe what I saw…

Example/Guide Answer

I looked out the window and couldn't believe what I had seen. Everywhere I looked, there was nothing but white snow blanketing the ground. The roads were covered in a thick layer of ice, and all the trees had been transformed into works of art with their branches layered with glittering icicles. It was like a magical wonderland outside, so much different than any other day before.

I wanted to leave bed immediately and explore this new winter wonderland. I wanted to throw snowballs at my siblings, build a giant snowman, and make snow angels everywhere! Playing in that fluffy white blanket seemed so exciting; it was like something from a dream come true!

I quickly dressed and went outside, taking in all the beauty I could never have imagined, even just an hour earlier. Everywhere around me looked like a winter wonderland! Everything was painted in white; trees were frosted with a sparkly coating of glistening snowflakes. Even though it was cold, I was mesmerised by how peaceful and serene it all looked, so much so that the chill didn't bother me.

The air smelled fresh and crisp, making everything feel even more special, while soft flakes fell from the sky like little cotton balls. Children laughed as they built their first snowman whilst others threw snowballs or made angels out of them for fun. It felt magical!

CREATIVE WRITING NUMBER 83

You find a mysterious treasure map. How would you start your treasure hunt?

Example/Guide Answer

I was shocked when I stumbled upon the mysterious treasure map. It was inside an old wooden box in the attic, covered with dust and cobwebs like it had been there for years. The parchment paper of the map was worn thin, but I could still make out its details: a skull symbol right in the middle and a winding path surrounding it that seemed to lead deeper into the woods.

I wanted to know if this could be real. Was there treasure hidden somewhere out there? My heart raced with excitement as images of gold coins and jewels flashed through my mind. I couldn't wait to start my treasure hunt. I had read stories about famous adventurers and their exciting adventures, searching for lost treasures. I wanted to be just like them, finding treasures of my own. So, I decided to create a treasure hunt of my own.

That night, I gathered some supplies - an empty bag for carrying food, a flashlight, water bottle - then plotted my route on the map before slipping out into the darkness. I stepped outside tentatively, looking around for any sign of parents or neighbours that might catch me in the act of exploration. The air was still, save for the crickets chirping in harmony with each other as if they were sending me on my way with their songs. Assured that no one else was awake, I took off into the woods with enthusiasm and excitement coursing through every inch of me.

CREATIVE WRITING NUMBER 84

You've got a magic pen. What can it do and how will you use it?

Example/Guide Answer

Growing up, I was always fascinated by the thought of having a magical pen. As a child, I would spend hours trying to craft the perfect stories and illustrate them with my trusty ballpoint pens. But my dreams were bigger than that. I wanted something that could do more than write words—I wanted something magical! I could bring all kinds of fantastical creations to life with an enchanted pen.

I could use the pen to make myself invisible to explore places without anyone noticing me. It would be great fun to sneak around and take pictures of things I have yet to see. Of course, another way to use the magical pen is to draw money whenever needed; this would make shopping trips much easier and more exciting! And with all the extra money, I can help those less fortunate than myself.

Finally, if none of those options sticks out right away, my magical pen could create beautiful artwork with each stroke across a canvas. My imagination ran wild, imagining what kind of things this magical pen could do. It could create delicious food with each stroke onto a plate or even make intricately crafted jewellery from scratch! I'm so excited to use this pen for all sorts of things.

CREATIVE WRITING NUMBER 85

You get to build your own dream treehouse. Describe what it's like.

Example/Guide Answer

My dream treehouse would be the most fantastic place in the world! It would be built high up in a tall tree with many branches. I can imagine spending hours in it, playing and exploring with my friends. The treehouse will have multiple levels connected by winding staircases and rope bridges. On the top level, I'll have a lookout point where I can sit and watch birds flying around me.

Inside, there will be cosy nooks for us to relax in as well as plenty of shelves for books and toys. I'll even install a refrigerator to store snacks for when we get hungry. My dream treehouse is sure to become our favourite spot to hang out together - it's going to be an adventure every day!

My dream treehouse is sure to be a magical hideaway where I can spend hours with my friends. It will likely be nestled in the branches of an old oak tree, with a ladder leading up to a cosy platform that looks out over the backyard. We'll bring beanbags and pillows to curl up on the deck and watch the clouds drift by in the sky. Inside, there'll be plenty of cushions to lie on while we tell each other stories, play pretends games, and make up imaginative adventures! If our parents let us, we could even put an old TV inside to watch our favourite films.

CREATIVE WRITING NUMBER 86

Write a story that includes the sentence, "I should have seen this coming."

Example/Guide Answer

My friends and I had always been inseparable growing up. We could always be found together, playing in the park or just walking around our neighbourhood with nothing to do but laugh and explore. This day was no different; we were headed for a walk when my friend suggested a detour to the ice cream shop down the street. I should have seen this coming.

The moment we stepped into the store, I knew it was a bad idea; it smelled like sugar and sticky hands everywhere! Despite my gut instinct telling me otherwise, I decided to join them in getting an ice cream cone. To say that things got messy would be an understatement—I ended up with more of it on my face than in my mouth! As they all laughed at me, I felt embarrassed; how had I allowed myself to get talked into something like this?

CREATIVE WRITING NUMBER 87

You have a magic wand. What spells will you cast?

Example/Guide Answer

If I had a magic wand, I would be the happiest kid in the world! The first spell I'd cast would be to make sure everyone has enough food. No one should ever go hungry.

My second spell would be to create a magical playground where everyone can play and have fun regardless of age or disability. It would also have an enchanted library full of books that could take you anywhere you wanted to go.

My third spell would give me the power to make wishes come true for anyone who needs help or encouragement. If someone were sad, I would be able to make them laugh with a special happy spell. And if somebody needed courage, I could grant them extra strength with just a few words and a wave of my wand. With my magical powers, there's no limit to what we can do together.

CREATIVE WRITING NUMBER 88

Describe a mistake you made and what you learned from it.

Example/Guide Answer

One of my biggest mistakes was not listening to my parents. One day, I decided to explore a nearby town with some friends without telling my parents. I left our house sneakily, and no one knew where I was going. I lost my friends and couldn't find my way home when it got dark. I was so scared and helpless. The sun was setting, and I had been lost for hours.

Luckily, an explorer found me and helped me find the main road. He smiled at me with kindness in his eyes and asked if he could help me find my way home. I nodded eagerly, relieved to have someone that knew what they were doing on my side. We set off together, following a path of branches laid out by the explorer as we travelled deeper into the woods towards the main road, I needed to take home. My parents were very disappointed but relieved when they saw me unharmed.

I learned that I always need to listen to and obey my parents because they know more than me and are making decisions for what is best for me. Hearing the consequences of my actions was hard, but it helped me understand why listening and respecting them is essential. Since then, I have done everything possible to show them how grateful I am for their guidance and love by following their instructions so they can trust me again like before. Looking back now, I can see how following their advice could have saved me from trouble and disappointment.

CREATIVE WRITING NUMBER 89

Write a speech that tells the whole school why you should be a student leader.

Example/Guide Answer

Good morning, everyone. I am here to tell you why I should be your next student leader. I'm here today to tell you why I should be a student leader. Being a leader means you are responsible for setting an example for the whole school and ensuring everyone is doing their best. As someone who has been involved with our school for many years, I understand how important it is to have a strong role model in this position.

I would make a great student leader because of my passion and enthusiasm for our school. Every day, I strive to make sure that each activity or task is completed with excellence and pride so that we can all look back at the end of the year, knowing we did our very best.

In addition, I have great ideas for projects we can do together as a school. Last week, my classmates and I organised a fun event for everyone where we raised money for charity and ensured everyone was having a fantastic time. It was indeed one of the most rewarding experiences of my life! We could do similar events if elected as a student leader.

CREATIVE WRITING NUMBER 90

If I could visit another planet, I would go to... Why?

Example/Guide Answer

If I could visit another planet, I would go to Jupiter! It's big, mysterious and looks so pretty on our planet Earth. I'm sure there are lots of exciting things to explore on Jupiter.

First, it has the most moons of any other planet in our Solar System, and one of them is named Europa – that sounds cool! Some huge storms on the planet include swirling clouds with intense winds and lightning, which is super cool to witness. Not only that, but Jupiter is a gas giant made up mostly of hydrogen and helium – two gases you don't get to see very often here on Earth!

If I visited Jupiter, there'd be something new around every corner. I'd likely find an alien race living beneath its surface or find evidence of life forms that once lived there.

There's so much potential to explore on Jupiter compared to any other place in space; surprises could be waiting everywhere. From vast oceans under the red-orange skies to volcanoes erupting with smoke - imagine how magical it must look!

CREATIVE WRITING NUMBER 91

You're the teacher for the day. What will you do in your lesson?

Example/Guide Answer

Today, I am the teacher for the day! This is exciting, and I can't wait to plan my first lesson. To kick off the day, I know just what I can do. First, we will start with fun activities like freeze dancing or charades. We can all get up and move around while having many laughs together.

Next, I will talk about something that everyone is interested in discussing, and that's their favourite book they read recently. We'll go around in a circle, and every student gets to share something they learned from that book or what they liked most about it.

Afterwards, we can play some games related to our discussion topics, such as a quiz show or skill-building activities like writing a summary or researching the characters in the story.

Being the teacher for the day was an amazing experience for me! It has made me realise exactly what teachers go through every day to help us learn more about ourselves and the world around us. Thank you so much for giving me this wonderful opportunity; I will never forget today!

CREATIVE WRITING NUMBER 92

You get to spend the night in a museum. What kind of museum? How will you have fun?

Example/Guide Answer

I am so excited! I get to spend the night in a museum. My parents decided it would be an amazing experience and a great way to explore knowledge and culture. The museum they chose is an art museum. With its high ceilings, and large walls of paintings, sculptures, photographs, and other art objects, it's like an artist's dream come true!

I can't wait to explore the different galleries filled with never-ending beauty. I am sure my eyes will sparkle with excitement when I see all the unique works of art in this place. We plan on having fun by playing hide-and-seek behind sculptures or pretending to be famous artists from the past while admiring our favourite pieces of work. It'll be like taking a journey through time!

To make it even better, we get to bring our sleeping bags and pillows so we can afterwards gaze up at the stars from inside the museum before going to sleep. We can bring our food and snacks for dinner if we like!

CREATIVE WRITING NUMBER 93

You dig the world's deepest hole. What lies at the bottom?

Example/Guide Answer

I love a good challenge. My friends and I were determined to dig the world's deepest hole. We worked for months, digging with shovels and pickaxes, competing against each other to see who could remove the most dirt. After gruelling labour, we reached an incredible depth of over 100 feet! It was a fantastic accomplishment.

At the bottom of our deep hole, we found something completely unexpected; a secret chamber filled with ancient artefacts from thousands of years ago! We had unearthed an archaeological site that had remained undiscovered until now. As we explored further into this unknown space, I couldn't believe my eyes when I saw all the incredible things hidden down there: old books written in languages that none of us knew, coins and jewellery made from materials that are no longer used today; and even statues depicting mythical creatures such as dragons!

CREATIVE WRITING
NUMBER 94

You get to change the school uniform. What would you make everyone wear and why?

Example/Guide Answer

I always dreamed of getting to pick out the school uniform for everyone. That dream has become a reality, and I feel like a king with all the choices! I would make everyone wear shoes that light up when you walk. Not only will they look cool, but they'll also be practical when it gets dark. Also, they can help us have fun while we stay safe on the way home from school.

For our shirts, I'd choose something with bright colours that will only fade slowly, even after washing and wearing over and over again throughout the school year. That way, our uniforms are always looking neat! We could match this with comfortable trousers in basic black or navy blue; these will never go out of style and look great on anyone.

The uniform needs to fit every season too! For winter months, I'd pick jumpers, jackets, and jeans so we can stay warm while looking stylish. For summer, shorts and t-shirts will keep us cool during hot days at school. And it would be great if there were skirts or dresses too - so girls have more choice in what they wear each day!

CREATIVE WRITING NUMBER 95

If you could invent anything, what would it be?

Example/Guide Answer

I used to dream of inventing something to make life easier and more fun. I wanted something that would change the world and be unique. I thought of inventing a machine that instantly turned any food into ice cream. This way, everyone could have their favourite flavour without buying it from the shop.

The machine could recognise different ingredients by scanning them with a built-in scanner. It then turns those ingredients into delicious ice cream in seconds! Also, it comes with many other toppings you can choose from, so you can customise your unique treat every time. This invention would make me feel like a genius since no one else has ever thought about it.

Imagine how awesome it would be to have an ice cream machine in my own home. I could get delicious desserts whenever I wanted! I could make exciting flavours, too - anything from creamy vanilla to tangy lemon ice cream would be possible. Anyone who came over would be so impressed by my incredible invention.

CREATIVE WRITING NUMBER 96

If I could have any job in the world, it would be…

Example/Guide Answer

If I could have any job in the world, it would be working with animals. Animals were always my favourite thing to learn about and care for, so it would be a dream come true if I got to make it my career.

Growing up, I spent all my free time playing with our neighbourhood cats and learning more about different kinds of wild animals. Every day after school, I would go outside and watch birds fly around or try to observe squirrels running up trees.

It was like having my zoo right outside of the house.

When thinking about what kind of job I'd want as an animal expert someday, a veterinarian came to mind. It would be so cool if I could help injured animals get better by using medicine or even surgery.

I love animals! Whenever I see an injured animal, I want to help them out. I would like to use medicine and even surgery to improve them. Imagine being able to take care of a sick animal and making sure they get back to its healthy life again.

CREATIVE WRITING NUMBER 97

Write a story that takes place in a forest.

Example/Guide Answer

I walked in the forest with my family on a hot summer day. Everything was peaceful and quiet under the shade of the tall trees. Beautiful birds sang their songs, and butterflies fluttered from one flower to the next. It was like stepping into another world. The sunshine barely made it through all the leaves, turning everything into dappled green light.

The smell of pine needles filled the air and gave off a sweet perfume mixed with all the other scents of nature. Walking further into the forest felt cooler and darker than outside - like stepping into another world. We stopped to take pictures of plants we spotted along our journey, finding many different kinds that were so vibrant and alive compared to those in our backyard.

We decided to rest by a little stream running through the forest's centre. We laid our picnic blanket on a soft grassy patch nearby and enjoyed snacks while dipping our feet in the cool running water. The tranquillity of this place was magical; I felt so at ease, surrounded by nature's beauty. After lunch, we explored further, looking for any interesting creatures or plants that we could find.

CREATIVE WRITING NUMBER 98

An alien arrives at your house. What happens next?

Example/Guide Answer

The other night I was alone in my room when I heard a loud banging at the door. At first, I thought it was just a weird noise from outside, but the door suddenly opened. I was standing there before I was an alien that had come to our house. It had one eye, two arms and three legs with bright green skin. I was so scared that I wanted to scream, but all that came out of my mouth were squeaks.

I shouted for my mum, and she appeared in the doorway, just as shocked! She carefully walked towards the alien and asked who he was and why he had come here. The alien replied with a strange language that neither of us understood, but then he showed her something in his hands which lit up like a star.

The alien seemed friendly enough because it began to talk in a strange language and waved its hands around as if trying to tell me something. After some time, we learned how to communicate, and it started telling me about life on its planet. It said things like they didn't have cars or TV, but instead, they had animals like giant flying cats! It sounded like such a cool place.

CREATIVE WRITING NUMBER 99

What is your favourite season and why?

Example/Guide Answer

My favourite season has always been summer. It's just such an exciting and fun time of year; the days are longer, there's sunshine everywhere, and everyone is much happier. I love going outside and playing all day without worrying about school or homework. The weather is perfect for playing tag with my friends on the playground and enjoying some ice cream from the truck that comes around in our area every day after school. We can also have picnics in the park, bike rides around town, or even take trips to the beach.

Summer is also great because it means family holidays. We drive out of town and explore different places every summer, which I love doing. Visiting new sites, hiking in nature preserves, swimming in lakes- it's like an adventure every time.

CREATIVE WRITING NUMBER 100

Describe the saddest day in your life. Why?

Example/Guide Answer

The saddest day of my life was last summer when I had to say goodbye to my best friend, who had moved away. We were inseparable, and even though I knew it would happen at some point, it still felt like a giant punch in the gut when she left. We'd been friends since kindergarten and shared so many fun memories. As we hugged each other tightly, I could feel tears streaming down my face, mixing with my best friend's. Even though she was only moving an hour away, it felt like the end of an era and knowing that our friendship would never be quite the same again made me incredibly sad.

I remember when we first became friends - she was so shy, but I could tell there were depths to her that no one else had noticed. Since then, we've shared all our deepest secrets and dreams - we even made a pinkie swear never to keep anything from each other! Knowing that our friendship will never be quite the same again makes me sad; no more sleepovers, movie nights, or days spent at the beach together. Now that she's moving away, everything will change, and I'm afraid to say goodbye.

THANK YOU

Thank you for purchasing our book.

Writing a book has been a fantastic experience for us. We have put countless hours of work into creating our masterpiece, and people are taking time out of their day to read it is incredibly humbling. We sincerely appreciate everyone who takes a chance on our book and purchases a copy.

As authors, we want to hear feedback about the book, so we know how to improve it for future projects. If you had the opportunity to read our book, please give us your honest opinion by providing a review about it. It does not matter if it is positive or negative, just if it is genuine and from your heart. Your words will help shape how we write in the future, so thank you in advance for taking this extra step!

Would you like to book a trial lesson for Maths and English?

The trial lesson will provide an opportunity for you and your child to interact with our staff. This allows us to understand each student's unique needs and develop targeted learning plans based on their individual requirements.

Contact us to discuss this further or to book a slot.

ABOUT SIMPLIFIED EDUCATION

In the age of digital technology, parents are increasingly looking for ways to provide their children with educational resources. Our company has stepped up to meet that need by offering a wide range of learning tools and activities specifically designed for kids at home.

Finding quality educational material for young children can take a lot of work. Many resources available require extra supervision or parental involvement that not all parents have enough time or energy to provide. We understand these struggles and are here to help!

Our team has developed an array of educational materials tailored explicitly for learning at home, ensuring kids stay engaged and continue the development of important skills.

BOOK YOUR FREE TRIAL NOW!

facebook.com/SimplifiedEducation

Copyright © 2023 by Simplified Education

All rights reserved.

No part of this book may be reproduced in any form or by any electronic or mechanical means, including information storage and retrieval systems, without written permission from the author, except for the use of brief quotations in a book review.

www.simplified-education.co.uk

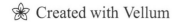 Created with Vellum